Y0-BRK-258

Date Due

12-6

1 -17

FORM 23 R   CR-212

JNS92-0414

$ 2.00

Here Is Your Hobby:
SKIING

The big attraction to skiing is primarily the fun it offers, and secondarily the challenge to develop and improve your skill on skis. The author is a strong advocate of skiing fundamentals and stresses the basic points, thus cutting through the confusion about the various "systems" of skiing. He explains about selecting and handling equipment, stresses the early development of helpful habits, and then progresses smoothly from walking on skis to ski jumping and cross-country racing.

HERE IS YOUR HOBBY...

SKIING

By
WILLIAM
FOSS

G. P. Putnam's Sons   New York

To Dulcie

© 1964 by William O. Foss

All Rights Reserved

Published simultaneously in the Dominion of
Canada by Longmans Canada Limited, Toronto
Library of Congress Catalog Card Number: 64-24562

MANUFACTURED IN THE UNITED STATES OF AMERICA

CONTENTS

Other books by William O. Foss
(with Erik Bergaust):

COAST GUARD IN ACTION
HELICOPTERS IN ACTION
MARINE CORPS IN ACTION

The HERE IS YOUR HOBBY books:

If you ask me why I ski, I can give a simple answer: "Because it's fun."

Skiing is indeed fun, because it is a healthy outdoor activity that can be enjoyed by novice as well as expert. Today, millions of Americans, men and women, boys and girls, are skiing and having fun doing it.

But skiing is more than fun. It's a challenge to constant improvement.

No skier, not even an expert, can say he knows everything there is to know about skiing.

Skiing is a sport that calls for improvements and more improvements; yet for all its demands, millions of people accept the challenge.

The racer who navigates at high speed through the tricky gates of the slalom course is not satisfied with his performance — even if he wins the race. He knows he could have shaved his time by one-tenth of a second if he hadn't made that unsatisfactory approach to the hairpin gate.

The ski jumper who has just completed a beautiful 250-foot leap knows he could have improved his spectacular performance. With more drive at the take-off, he could have gained a couple of additional feet.

The novice skier, who has just schussed down the training hill without making a sitzmark, knows he could have made a better run if he'd been more relaxed and hadn't spread his feet so far apart.

It is this challenge to improve his performance that stimulates and entices the skier to seek out adventure and comradeship on the white-faced slopes.

The purpose of this book is to whet your appetite for a challenging hobby: Skiing. You'll find it an easy sport to learn, but don't be deluded by the idea that you can become an expert skier by just reading this or any other ski-instruction book. Only by energetic and diligent practice can you become proficient on skis.

Accept the challenge, and have fun skiing.

WILLIAM O. FOSS

Beltsville, Maryland

HERE IS YOUR HOBBY...

SKIING

By WILLIAM FOSS

State of New Hampshire photo

American resorts offer some of world's finest ski conditions. These young skiers have fun skiing at Gunstock in Laconia-Gilford, New Hampshire.

1

Skiing Equipment

Skiing is one of the most exhilarating and relaxing sports; but to enjoy it as a hobby or as a competitive sport, you must have proper equipment.

Your skiing equipment needn't be expensive. Many newcomers to skiing make the mistake of buying extremely expensive equipment during the early stages of their skiing indoctrination. Expensive skiing equipment can wait until you become more proficient.

You can enjoy skiing just as much with lower-priced equipment — provided your skis, boots, and bindings are of good quality, design, and fit. You'll be able to purchase good, inexpensive equipment in most ski shops.

There's very little difference in the equipment necessary for men and women, except that women may prefer slightly shorter and lighter skis than men.

The selection of proper skiing equipment will require careful consideration. What you buy will, of course, depend upon your budget and individual preference. But be sure you know what you need before you invest in skiing equipment.

Boots

Few skiers realize how important it is to wear a good pair of proper-fitting ski boots; it is your boots and not your feet that guide the skis. As your body shifts, the boots transmit this force to the skis, enabling you to execute the many exciting skiing maneuvers.

When buying ski boots, try them on over a pair of heavy ski socks. After you've laced the boot, your heel should settle securely back into the heel of the boot. The boot should feel reasonably snug, but not tight. You should be able to wiggle your toes; they should barely touch the toe of the boot. Firm, well-built boots, high enough to come well above your ankles, will give your feet and ankles extra support.

Since leather stretches, it's better to buy boots that fit rather than loose boots. Comfortable-fitting boots are apt to become loose-fitting after they've been broken in.

Miller Ski Co. photo
This type of safety binding releases toe under the pressure of a fall.

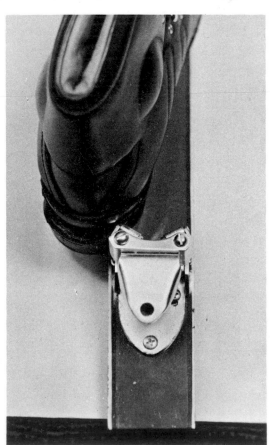

14

Lace your boots so they are molded firmly — but not tightly — to your feet. If the boots are laced too tight, your feet will get cold from lack of circulation.

While it's a pleasant sight to see a chivalrous young man lace the boots of a lady skier, the lady would be better off to lace her own boots. The heavy-handed male may lace them too tight.

Give your ski boots the same care you would any other quality shoes. With good care, ski boots will last several years.

Do *not* oil your ski boots; instead, use a good grade of boot grease or ordinary shoe polish containing wax.

After skiing, stuff the boots with newspapers or rags to absorb the moisture. Wet boots shouldn't be dried too quickly, or the leather will stiffen. Also, soles should never be brought in direct contact with a hot stove or radiator.

Always remember that ski boots are for skiing only. Don't use them for walking.

Skis

Most skis today are designed for special purposes, and they are made of wood, metal, plastic, and fiberglass.

The strongest and most durable wooden skis are made of laminated wood. Strips of wood, usually ash or hickory, or a mixture of both, are bonded together to form strengthened billets which are shaped into skis. Hickory skis are highly recommended, since hickory is 35 percent stronger than ash.

Wooden skis should be equipped with steel edges for better control when turning or skiing on icy snow. Steel edges also cut wear on wooden skis.

Metal skis cost more than wooden skis, but they're popular because they require practically no maintenance during non-skiing months. Metal skis are more maneuverable than wooden skis, thereby making skiing easier and less tiring. But they don't track well on hard snow, and at high speeds they can make skiing somewhat difficult for the novice.

As the ski industry continues to make technological advances, improved metal skis, along with those made of new plastics and fiberglass, are entering the market.

15

ONTARIO COOPERATIVE LIBRARY SYSTEM

For everyday skiing, combination skis — so called because they can be used for slalom, downhill, and touring — are favored by recreational skiers. The beginner should learn the mastery of skiing on combination skis.

Slalom skis are narrower and shorter than combination skis, and are easier to turn on hard-packed snow.

For downhill skiing, which calls for high speeds, racers use longer and heavier skis. Downhill skis are wider than slalom skis.

Since there is very little turning in cross-country skiing, cross-country skis are extremely narrow, light, and flexible.

Ski jumping requires longer and heavier skis. While other skis have one groove, jumping skis are designed with three grooves on the bottom. The extra grooves aid in steering a straight course.

What's the correct length for you to be safe in all snow conditions? The skis should be long enough to reach to the middle of the palm when your arm is raised straight above your head. Women may prefer relatively shorter skis, but they should never reach lower than the base of their hand.

Longer skis give you faster speed and firmer steering on a straight run. But the beginner will find they're harder to turn

Miller Ski Co. photo

This typical safety ski binding releases heel when twisting force is unsafe.

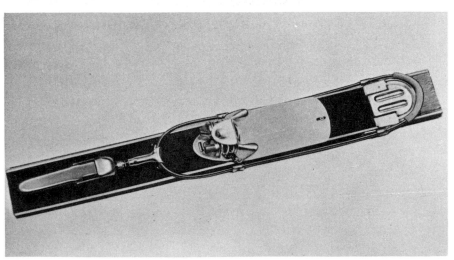

than are shorter skis. If your skis are too short, though, they'll tire you quickly, because they require more movement of your leg muscles to keep them under control.

When selecting your skis, be sure they're not warped. You can do this by placing the bottom of one ski against that of the other and pressing the skis together. They meet the test if they are equal in length and if all points of the gliding surfaces touch.

The groove on the bottom of the ski has to be exactly in the middle and absolutely straight. To check the straightness of the groove, hold the ski by its tip and sight down the running surface. Avoid skis with uneven grooves.

All skis are built with an arch — or camber — in the middle. This is to distribute weight evenly when you are skiing. When ski bottoms are placed together, this camber should measure 1½ to 2 inches. If the arch is too great, your skis will be difficult to turn. With too little arch, skis will sag in the middle, making them wander and hard to control.

Your skis will give you years of excellent service if you follow these simple rules:

Clean the skis off after each ski trip. Stand them on their tips to allow melting snow to run off completely, and never place skis near stoves and furnaces.

During summer months, store your skis in a dry place. Strap the skis with running surfaces together and with a wooden block spreading them apart at the middle. This will maintain the camber. A spreader between the ski tips will also maintain the bend when the skis are not in use.

Bindings

Good bindings are important; they hold your boots to the skis. Bindings should be strong, safe, and easily adjustable. They should make your ski boots fit firmly in the toe irons, with no side play on the skis.

Release bindings are recommended for all skiers, except that racers and ski jumpers, because of the nature of their specialty, use different bindings. Release bindings reduce the possibility

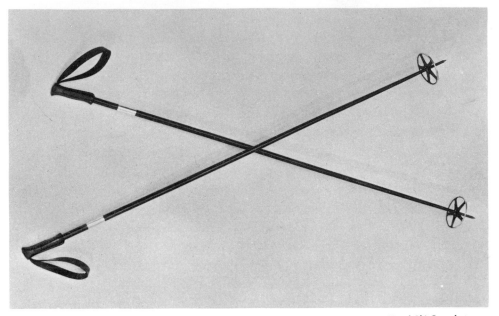

Head Ski Co. photo

Ski poles should be long enough to reach from ground to armpits and should have small, light rings and wide straps.

of injury. If pressure on the foot becomes excessive, as happens in a fall, the foot is separated from the ski.

There are hundreds of types of safety bindings, so your selection is largely a matter of personal taste. Just be sure, before you buy safety bindings, that you understand thoroughly their mechanism. Better safety bindings have few moving parts and are simple to adjust.

Poles

Ski poles may be made of tubular steel or aluminum, fiberglass, bamboo, or cane. They help your balance, keep you from slipping when skiing uphill, and help you push to greater speeds when skiing downhill. They can also be used as braking devices.

Your ski poles should be long enough to reach from the floor to your armpits. Longer poles will hamper your downhill skiing; shorter poles will make it difficult to climb hills.

Pole straps should fit firmly around your wrists. Wide straps are most comfortable.

Rings at the bottom of the poles prevent them from sinking into the snow. Rings, or baskets, as they are also called, should be small and light; large rings are clumsy.

Waxing

Before you go skiing, you must wax the running surfaces of your skis. Wax protects wood and makes skis slicker and easier to glide over the snow. All skis, with the possible exception of certain plastic-bottom skis, should be waxed.

Waxing can become a sticky subject with skiers; everybody seems to have his own idea on what constitutes proper waxing. Racers are most fussy about waxing, for the type of wax and how it is applied can mean the difference between victory and defeat.

While there are waxes for almost every conceivable snow and weather condition, the average skier will do well if he sticks with three basic waxes: 1) liquid, painted on as a base; 2) hard, for cold, dry snow; and 3) soft for melting, wet snow.

These waxes can be bought separately, but many manufacturers now sell waxing kits containing all three basic waxes, plus cork and brush for spreading and polishing.

Clothing

Clothing is largely a matter of individual taste. Ski pants, sweaters, parkas, mittens, and gloves should be warm, windproof, and water repellent. Avoid heavy and bulky clothes; they will only hamper your movements and tire you quickly. Exercising with too much clothing will make you perspire, and if you start removing garments in the cold air, you stand a good chance of getting chilled.

Mittens are warmer than gloves, but gloves give you greater control of your poles.

Wear no more than two pairs of ski socks. Otherwise you'll cramp your toes and cut off circulation.

To prevent your ears from freezing, wear a headband or similar headgear.

Ski goggles, with dark lenses to prevent your eyes from getting inflamed or snowblind, are important accessories.

2

Learning to Ski

Skiing is a hobby that can be enjoyed by people of all ages. The earlier you learn to ski, the more proficient you'll become and the longer you'll enjoy this wonderful winter outdoor activity. Youngsters have the physical requirements for skiing: they're agile, and they have body rhythm, which is so essential to the makings of an expert skier. They're also alert and daring — qualities that separate champions from ordinary skiers.

Learning to ski is simple, but some people say it's complicated. They point out that there are so many different systems in skiing that the beginning skier is apt to become confused and discouraged.

There are, of course, many techniques of skiing taught by various American ski schools. What they boil down to is this: they're variations and improvements of basic skiing techniques.

In this book we'll concentrate on fundamentals. The knowledge of these fundamentals should cut confusion and should enable the beginner to ski well in the shortest possible time.

Learning to ski is simply learning to keep your balance on a pair of wooden sticks. At first they'll feel awkward and clumsy.

U. S. Forest Service photo

Starting out for slopes of Winter Park Ski Area, Arapaho National Forest, Colorado, these skiers show right way to carry skis.

But after a few hours of practice you'll find you can master and control the skis with ease.

Always remember that skiing is a sport — a game — so treat your skiing lessons as a game in which you aim to have fun.

Don't be in a hurry to catch up with the experts who are having such great fun swooshing downhill at a fast clip. First learn the basic maneuvers — and learn them accurately. A sloppy skier won't amount to much, and he'll never have much fun.

A word of caution: when you get tired, stop skiing.

Before starting out on your first skiing lesson, it's wise to master the art of carrying your skies. At ski resorts, all skiers — including girls — are expected to carry their own skis. Improper handling of skis can make you a menace. One quick way to lose friends is to clobber them in the head with a pair of hickory sticks.

Carry skis over your shoulder, bottoms together, tips forward and down, supported by one hand. Carry poles in the other hand. To help support the skis, lay the poles over your free shoulder, crossing them under the skis behind your neck.

Indoors, or when going in and out of buildings, carry your skis and ski poles vertically.

The day you learned to walk, you took a big step forward in life. When you learn to walk on skis, you take the most important step toward becoming a skier.

Walking is the simplest and most important movement in skiing. In the walking maneuver, you learn balance, correct body position, coordination, and rhythm.

To learn skiing safely, start the walking maneuver on level ground. Sliding downhill is exciting, but hills can wait till you can handle yourself safely on level ground.

Walking on skis is somewhat like the walking you're accustomed to. On skis, you really don't walk, though — you glide your skis over the snow.

With the poles at your side, start your walking exercise by moving your feet in a regular walking manner. Knees should be

Robert St. Louis photo

To walk on skis, bend knees and lean body forward with most of weight over advanced ski as it slides on snow. Bring opposite pole forward. Keep sliding skis alternately ahead of each other.

24

bent and flexible, body leaning forward. Most of your weight should be over the advanced ski as it slides.

Advance the right ski with the left pole, the left ski with the right pole, and so on. Put the poles in the snow just a little ahead of the bindings and push. While pushing you ahead, the poles help you maintain balance. Keep your elbows close to your body — it gives you good leverage.

After learning to walk with the aid of ski poles, walk without them. Skiing without poles will aid the beginner in learning proper transfer of body weight, balance, timing, and control of the skis.

When you practice walking on skis, keep up a steady forward impetus. Stay on level ground. But as you progress, move to a slight slope. When walking is slightly uphill, lift the skis off the snow and set them down hard after each forward motion to prevent backsliding.

When walking, don't look at your arms and legs; concentrate on watching where you're going. Later, when you advance to high-speed skiing, the safety of yourself and others will depend upon your alertness. So always keep your eyes open.

I can't stress too often that to ski properly you must retain proper bend and knee flexibility, always leaning your body forward. If you lean back, your weight shifts from the front to the rear of your skis. Then you're off balance, and the skis will slip away from under you. The end result is obvious: you fall.

The beginner can expect to take many falls, but even expert skiers fall. Skiing calls for split-second timing and coordination. The skier who's slightly off balance is apt to find himself carving out sitzmarks in the snow.

When you know you've lost your balance, try to control your fall. You have a split second in which to do so. Relax as you go down; try to fall sideways and to the rear, with knees and skis together. In a safe and controlled fall, body and skis are as far from each other as possible.

Many beginners have trouble getting up after a fall. There are simple ways of getting up.

First, arrange the skis so that they're parallel to each other and

Robert St. Louis photo

Even an expert skier can take a tumble. Knowing right way to get up is important.

Robert St. Louis photo

First step in getting up from a fall: place your skis across slope and parallel to one another.

Robert St. Louis photo

With free (downhill) hand, dig ski pole into snow behind you and pull yourself to ward handle. At same time, use other (uphill) hand to push yourself away from snow.

Robert St. Louis photo

Keep skis horizontally across slope to prevent their sliding forward or slipping backward.

on your downhill side. Keep them horizontal to prevent their sliding forward or slipping back.

Then, with the inside arm resting on the snow, push yourself away from the ground. Take the ski pole in your free hand (the one not resting against the snow) and dig it into the snow behind your back. With the inside arm resting against the snow, push yourself away from the ground. At the same time you pull yourself up with the ski pole.

In another method of arising from a fall, you start by sticking both poles together into the hill. Place one hand near the grips and the other down near the baskets, and then push yourself up and away from the hill.

As with other skiing fundamentals, falling gracefully and getting up quickly takes practice. The proper method is always the safest way.

3

Changing Direction

There are several methods of turning about. The simplest one is the *step turn*. While a step turn is best done on level ground, it can also be executed on a slight slope.

Start from a standing position, holding the poles slightly out of the snow. If you want to move to the right, lift the right ski's toe out of the snow and turn it to the right while the heel serves as the pivot. When you place the right ski back on the snow, your skis form a V. Bring the left ski alongside the right in the same manner. Repeat these movements until you face the direction you want to go.

If you want to change your direction to the left, you start out with the left ski, moving it to the left with the tail in the snow. When the V-angle is formed, bring the right ski out of the snow and place it parallel with the left. Repeat the steps until you're facing the desired direction.

You may also use the tip of the ski instead of the heel as a pivot point. This method is particularly useful when you want to change directions at a dead end or in a confined area.

Robert St. Louis photos

You're looking downhill at ski instructor Arthur G. Furrer as he starts kick turn to right. First step is to move right ski forward and upward.

Then he turns his body to the right, using heel of right ski as pivot to rotate the ski outward.

Kick Turn

For a fast turn around, the *kick turn* is the best method. It can be executed on level terrain and is essential for changing direction on a hill.

The kick turn looks difficult, and you might take a spill the first time you try it. Once you learn it, however, you'll use the kick turn a lot on the level and in climbing.

To execute the kick turn you start from a standing position with skis parallel. Stretch your arms out horizontally, and place the poles in the snow about 18 to 24 inches in front of the toes of your ski boots.

To make a kick turn to the right, lift or kick the right ski forward and upward until the ski is perpendicular, its heel alongside

30

the tip of the left ski. In order to get good force behind your right leg, bring it back slightly before making the kick, in much the same way a football player executes a drop kick.

Next, turn your body to the right. Use the tail of the right ski as a pivot, rotate the ski outward and bring it down parallel to the left ski. You are now in the awkward position of having your skis pointing in opposite directions.

To get out of this twisted position and complete the turn, shift your weight to your right ski, and bring the left ski and pole around and alongside the right ski.

Now you have completed a 180-degree turn.

When you have mastered the kick turn on level ground, move to a slight slope, then to a steep hill. A kick turn on a slope or hill is executed in the same way it is on level ground, except that the downhill (lower) ski is turned first. Then if you should lose your balance you won't fall downhill without having some control over your fall.

When making a kick turn on a slope or hill, be certain you are standing horizontally across the hill; otherwise your skis may go out from behind you.

Now you're looking uphill at the same kick turn to right. At this stage, skis point awkwardly in opposite directions.

Turn to right is completed by shifting weight to right foot and bringing left ski and pole around and alongside right ski.

The beginning skier should put much practice into the kick turn. It's an excellent skiing maneuver that requires good coordination of arms and legs and a strong sense of balance. For conditioning your leg muscles and improving your balance, try making kick turns without the aid of poles.

Later, when you have become a proficient skier, you may want to try the *jump turn* without help of poles. To make a jump turn you crouch low, keeping knees and feet close together, and straighten up suddenly, twisting the upper part of your body at the same time in the desired direction. This must be done with considerable force so that the skis will follow the turning body. During the jump turn, the skis are off the ground. Land in a crouch to absorb the shock. Carry poles loosely.

Instructor Furrer shows students how to make step turn, the simplest method of turning around on level ground or slight slope.

32

Robert St. Louis photo

4

Getting to the Top

Ski lifts have made it easy for skiers to get to the top of a hill. But the accessibility of ski lifts has also made many skiers lazy. A good skier not only knows how to glide down the hill, but he can also get to the top under his own power.

Climbing is work, of course, and the steeper the hill, the more work you must do. Size up the hill before you try to climb it. Decide what climbing steps will get you to the top with the least effort. A tired skier will miss the fun, and he may cause an accident to himself or others.

Begin by walking up the hill, using your poles for support in the same way as when walking on the level. On gentle slopes, slide the skis forward without lifting them from the snow.

As the slope becomes steeper, your glides become shorter. Lift the skis and slap them into the snow. This will give the skis better holding qualities. Dig the poles harder into the ground, not too far ahead and close to the skis. Keep your body forward at all times.

When you find yourself slipping backward, you must switch to one of the following climbing steps.

Side Step

Sidestepping is a simple way for student skiers to climb a hill. It is also useful for stepping sideways over logs, stumps, low fences, and other obstacles.

Begin the side step with your skis placed together and horizontally across the hill. Stamp the skis hard into the snow to prevent slipping. Place all your weight on your lower ski.

Lift your uphill ski and step sideways and upward, edging the upward ski into the snow as you stamp it down. Simultaneously with the leg movement, lift the upper pole and place it firmly into the snow above your upper ski; your weight now shifts to the upper ski.

Next you bring the downhill ski up and parallel with the upper ski. At the same time, you bring the lower pole up and put it down directly alongside your downhill ski.

This completes one cycle of the side step. To continue the climb, merely repeat the cycle.

Robert St. Louis photo

Students take lesson in sidestepping, a simple way to climb a hill.

Robert St. Louis photo
When climbing a slope with the diagonal side step, edge your skis firmly into the snow to prevent slipping.

Diagonal Side Step

The diagonal side step is another method of climbing when the hill gets too steep for going straight uphill. The diagonal side step is actually a combination of the basic walking step and the side step. Each diagonal side step takes you upward and forward across the hill.

The diagonal side step is actually easier to do than the regular side step. As in the side-step maneuver, you start with your skis horizontal across the hill, making sure your skis don't slip forward or backward.

The movement in the diagonal side-step maneuver is the same as the regular side step, except that the ski is moved forward about a foot or so with each step.

When advancing the skis during the diagonal side step, be sure the forward step isn't too great; otherwise you can lose your balance and fall.

While you can safely make big upward steps during the sidestep maneuver, it is advisable to make shorter steps when climbing the hill with the diagonal side step.

Edging is important when climbing with the diagonal side step. On a gentle slope, in soft snow, put your skis down firmly. When the snow is hard, edge the skis into the snow and lean your body away from the slope. This will force the edges to hold against the slope, with your weight in a vertical line over the skis.

You can make good speed traversing a hill with the diagonal side step. As you walk and sidestep up the hill, remember to make proper use of the poles.

To alter direction when climbing a hill with the diagonal side step you merely execute a perfect kick turn. I say "perfect," for if you don't, you'll fall.

The Herringbone

When the slope isn't too steep, you can get to the top quickly by doing the herringbone climb. While herringboning is quicker than sidestepping, it's also more tiring. Limit herringboning to short climbs and moderate slopes.

To begin the herringbone climb, you face uphill and spread your ski tips wide apart so that the skis form a V. Keep your weight well forward, bend your knees forward and inward so that the skis get good edging in the snow. This is a rather awkward position, but it prevents you from slipping backward.

Make the first step by placing your weight on one ski, raising the other slightly above the snow and moving it forward and upward. Then place this ski in the snow, edge it inward, and transfer your body weight to it. Then move the other ski in the same way and place it slightly ahead.

During the herringbone climb, you use the ski poles as you do in the walking step, except that you place them to the rear of your body and to the outside of each ski. For the best supporting leverage, put your hands on top of the ski poles.

Since herringboning is a tiring maneuver, you may want to change to a diagonal side step in order to complete the climb. To

Same situation viewed from back shows clearly how right ski has been advanced. Then left ski is moved up.

Robert St. Louis photos
Quick method of getting to top when slope is not too steep is demonstrated by Arthur G. Furrer.

do this, you plant both poles behind you to support your weight, then move the ski tips around until you have stepped into the desired position.

Or, if you want to go from a diagonal side step to a herringbone, you simply reverse the procedure: Move the upper ski in the desired direction, using its heel as a pivot point. Keep full body weight on this ski and edge it into the snow. Bring the other ski around in the same way. You will now be in a herringbone position. During the turn, hold both poles to the rear to brace your body.

37

Sun Valley News Bureau photo

These youngsters show good form as they follow the leader in a straight downhill run.

5

Straight Downhill Running

Once you've learned to walk on skis, change direction, and get up gracefully after falls, you're ready for straight downhill running.

Straight downhill skiing, which is also called schussing (from the German word *schuss,* meaning shot), is the fastest way to descend. It is also one of the most thrilling parts of skiing.

But, before concerning yourself about speed, you need to learn the fundamentals of downhill skiing. You start on a gentle slope and move to steeper hills as you gain skill and confidence.

Since straight downhill running means skiing without turning, select a gentle slope with a level runout at the bottom so that you can come to a natural stop without falling or turning. Make sure there are no obstacles in your way. Be alert for other skiers.

When you start, keep your skis close together, one a few inches ahead of the other. Relax your body, and bend forward slightly at the hips. Your knees are bent and pushed forward from your ankles; keep your heels flat on the skis. Your body and knees should be able to move up and down in an easy, elastic fashion.

Push forward with the poles, then let your arms hang loose, close to the knees. Keep the poles pointing to the rear, and don't let them drag in the snow.

Be relaxed and alert as you ski downhill. Look straight ahead, not at your ski tips. Bend your knees, and use them as shock absorbers.

You may be a little unstable during your first few trips down the hill. But after about 20 or more runs, you'll find straight downhill running an exhilarating experience.

To get the feel of the skis and to develop your balance, try some different running positions. For example, try downhill running without poles. Or go into a deep crouch, leaning your body forward and bending your knees deeper.

Try lifting your skis as you glide down the hill. When doing this exercise, shift your weight from one ski to the other. Tip of lifted ski should be slightly advanced.

For balance and coordination, try reaching down and picking up a glove as you ski downhill. As you improve, try picking up two gloves at the same time.

When schussing in soft snow, keep the skis close together; in hard snow they may be separated slightly.

6

Braking and Stopping

To enjoy the thrill of speeding downhill, you must know how and when to slow down or stop. Never take it for granted that other skiers will get out of your way when you come schussing downhill. Learning to brake and stop your descent should be your first order of business as soon as you've mastered straight downhill running on gentle slopes.

The safest and easiest braking and stopping maneuver in skiing is the *snowplow*. It's also one of the most significant fundamentals in skiing, being the take-off point for several important turns.

Practice the snowplow on a gentle hill, the same one on which you made your first straight downhill run.

With your skis in a downhill position, slowly force their tails outward and keep the tips together until the skis form a wide V. Keep your knees and ankles bent and flexed forward toward the tips.

With this maneuver, you can brake your descent or come to a complete halt. To control your downward speed, edge your skis inward. To stop, increase the bend in your knees and apply more edging.

Avoid looking at your ski tips. Look beyond the skis so you can see what's going on ahead.

If you make too wide a V maneuver, your ski tips are apt to cross, and then you may end up falling, the very thing a good snowplow will prevent you from doing.

During the snowplow maneuver, point the poles to the rear in a V, and use them only for balance.

The next move is to combine the downhill running maneuver with the snowplow. Start down the hill in a straight downhill run, then apply the snowplow braking maneuver, return to the straight running position, and come to a complete stop with the snowplow. Repeat this exercise until you can control your speed and your ability to stop at will.

Robert St. Louis photo

Knee action is stressed as these skiers practice the snowplow, the safest and easiest braking and stopping maneuver in skiing.

7

The Turns

Very few skiers, including the racers, ski downhill in a straight line. For a successful downhill run, the skier changes his direction and speed through a series of twists and turns. Not only is turning fun but often it's also absolutely necessary. Even if you should try to ski straight down a long hill, the shape of the hill — with its trees, bushes, and bumps — would force you to turn simply to avoid a collision or spill.

Although you learn the fundamentals of straight downhill running on gentle slopes, it would be foolhardy to try skiing straight down a steep hill. You can reach tremendous speeds on skis, and unless you're in complete control of the skis and yourself, your skiing efforts could end up disastrously.

There are many different turns in skiing. While most of them are generally easy and provide you with considerable fun, you can become a highly proficient skier by mastering relatively few basic turns.

Snowplow Turn

Having already learned to brake and stop your descent with the snowplow maneuver, you can easily make the snowplow turn your first controlled turn. The snowplow turn is the most elemental skiing turn; it is also the most useful.

To begin, place yourself in a straight downhill position, then switch over to the snowplow braking maneuver. To make a snowplow turn, you rotate your body in the direction you want to go.

To make a snowplow turn to the left, for instance, your body weight is transferred smoothly to the outside (right) ski by rotating your body and shoulder to the left. This shifting of body weight starts the turning action.

Robert St. Louis photo
Snowplow turn is most basic and most useful skiing turn. Start in snowplow braking position, rotate body the way you wish to turn, and shift weight to downhill ski.

Robert St. Louis photos
Front and rear views of snowplow show
skis properly edged and their toes brought
close together. Note position of poles.

45

If you don't turn immediately, your weight isn't on your outside ski.

The bend of your right knee is increased as the turn progresses. Your left knee is kept well bent with the ski flat and unweighted throughout the turn.

Keep the ski tips even and the V-angle of the skis constant throughout the turn.

Ski poles are used only for balance and are pointed sideward and back.

As you complete the turn, either place your body weight evenly on both skis to continue in a snowplow, or gradually transfer your weight to your left ski to start a turn to the right.

It is good practice to make a series of downhill runs, snowplow-turning alternately left and right, until you get thoroughly familiar with this elementary skiing turn. Soon you'll find you can ski down most slopes under perfect control.

The Traverse

Along with learning the snowplow turn, you must also practice the traverse, the position used for going down and across the hill.

Traversing is like straight running — schussing — downhill, except that you ski down and across the hill.

The starting position for the traverse is the same as that for straight downhill running: skis are parallel and close together, but the uphill ski is slightly advanced (about 4 inches or approximately half the length of your boot). Put most of your weight on the downhill ski. As you start the traverse run, lean your knees toward the hill and keep your upper body angled over the weighted lower ski. Your body will now have a position resembling a comma.

To prevent slipping, edge your skis into the hill. To do this, press your knees together and lean toward the hill. The more edging you apply, the more pronounced will be your comma position.

When traversing downhill, hold your ski poles as in a straight downhill position. You may, however, push on them slightly to help you cross the hill.

Stem Turn

What to do after you've completed a traverse run across the hill? You could stop, make a kick turn, and then traverse in the other direction down and across the hill. But you are obviously not going to come to a complete halt at the end of each traverse run. If you had to do that, you'd soon be discouraged with skiing. The answer is to make a stem turn.

Once you've mastered the snowplow turn, the stem turn becomes relatively simple; both turns are almost identical in body and leg movements.

The stem turn starts from a traverse position with skis parallel. Move the uphill ski into a stem position — that is, push the ski outward to form a V (this is almost like making a snowplow, except that you stem with one ski instead of two to form the V). Then shift your weight over to the stem ski. The weight will force you to go in the direction your skis are pointing. To complete the turn, swivel your hips and shoulders in the new direction, inward toward the turn, with a rotary motion.

The turn is completed on the lower ski (which was the uphill ski when you started the maneuver). In order to continue the traverse run, you must bring the inner ski parallel to the lower (stem) ski. Lift the inner ski slightly, bringing it parallel to the outer ski. This requires good coordination of body and legs.

Once you've completed a snowplow turn or a stem turn, say from left to right, complete another turn in the other direction.

Many skiers make the mistake of making their turns in one direction. They favor either the right or the left side. Shake off this habit early. Practice all turns in both directions. The more proficient you are, the more fun you'll get out of skiing.

Polish your snowplow turns and stem turns in all sorts of snow: icy, hard-packed, heavy and wet, and new and soft. Practice on various hills; try easy slopes first; then move to steeper ones.

Robert St. Louis photos

Instructor leads students in stem turn. From a traverse position with skis parallel . . .

. . . you bring uphill ski to a stem position by pushing it outward to form a V, and then shift weight to this ski.

Robert St. Louis photo

Body rotation, crouch, knee action, all combine to make perfect stem christie. There's less stem and more body movement in stem christie than in regular stem turn.

As you gain skill and confidence, you'll want to make faster stem turns. For more speed, simply reduce the time you hold the skis in a V position. In other words, the quicker you complete the stem turn, the faster will be your speed when you bring the skis back to a parallel position.

High-Speed Turns

Snowplow turns and stem turns are comparatively slow turns. But once you've mastered these basic turns, it's quite easy to move into high gear with the faster christiania (christie) and parallel turns. They're the most advanced turns in skiing and are executed with the basic motions already learned, such as forward lean, edge control and body movement.

The *stem christie* is one of the most commonly used christiania

Photo: Courtesy Penny Pitou Zimmerman

Correct form for traversing a slope is demonstrated by Olympic medalist Penny Pitou Zimmerman and Egon Zimmerman.

turns. It may be used on all slopes, at all speeds, and on all snows except very heavy, breakable crust. Racers as well as weekend skiers use the stem christie.

To do the stem christie, you start out in a traverse position. Approach your turn in a medium crouch position, knees well bent and forward. Stem the inside ski; that is, push it outward, so that ski tips are almost touching. Now twist your body, starting from feet and working up to the shoulders, transferring your weight to the stemmed outside ski. As your body rotates, slide the inside ski in parallel with the outside ski and somewhat ahead of it. The forward motion of your skis and your body rotation will enable you to complete the turn. Resume the crouch position for continuing descent.

Since the stem christie is executed in one continuous movement, coordination of the bent knees and rotating body becomes extremely important. The up-and-down motion of the body lightens the skis and allows them to skid into the turns.

50

Sun Valley News Bureau photo

A trio of expert skiers execute perfect parallel turns. In parallel turn, often called a pure christiania, you make turn from beginning to end with skis together.

Let your arms and poles swing with your body during the stem christie.

A *parallel turn* is what oldtime skiers call a *pure christiania*. It means simply that from the beginning of the turn to the end, your skis remain together in parallel position.

Parallel skiing down the fall line (the most direct downhill line) at high speed is the dream of every skier. It's done with very little stemming but with considerable body movement and shifting of weight from one ski to the other.

The parallel turn begins in a traverse position. Your body is in a crouch, knees well forward. Your inner ski is slightly ahead. As you approach the turn, you rotate your body in the same motion I just mentioned in describing the stem christie movement. But your body rotation is faster than it is in the stem christie. With the rotating body motion, transfer your weight to the outside ski, which is stemmed ever so slightly. Slide your inside ski parallel

51

with your outside ski, and then lean your body forward, away from the hill, to continue your speedy downhill flight.

You won't have been on the ski trail long before you hear skiers talk about doing the *wedeln*. This seems to be the ultimate goal of modern skiers, but don't try it before you've mastered the ski maneuvers I've already discussed.

Actually, there's nothing mysterious about the wedeln. It's simply skiing with the skis parallel and together at all times. While we now call it wedeln or fishtailing, not too many years ago we called it the wiggle, advanced parallel, or just plain zigzagging.

Call it what you will, but wedeln requires you to make quick parallel turns at all times. Skis are kept almost flat, but are edged with pressure of your knees. You don't stem, but use plenty of

Vermont Development Department photo

Wedeln technique is one of most exciting skiing maneuvers. Ski downhill with skis parallel and together at all times. Shifting of body weight and edging of skis produce zigzag maneuvering.

Robert St. Louis photos

To make hop turn, start with skis parallel, knees bent, body in crouch.

Jump upward, pull skis off ground, pivot around pole.

53

Land facing opposite direction, skis remaining parallel.

up-and-down motion to shift your weight from one ski to the other.

Wedeln requires excellent timing in the use of the poles. Before making a turn, bring your inside pole straight forward and touch it down slightly on the turn.

Jump Turns

When skiers meet obstacles, they must react fast. Sometimes a stem turn or parallel christie won't do the trick. Then you should either make a jump turn or execute a neat *gelandesprung* jump.

These maneuvers look difficult, but they're really not so tough as they appear. With a bit of practice, most agile skiers will be able to make these jump maneuvers in fine form.

To get the feel of jumping around with skis, first try the *hop turn*. This is a very simple exercise.

Robert St. Louis photo
Twist body around poles to accomplish jump turn.

Stand on a level spot, skis in parallel position. Then touch one pole down in the snow, bend down in a semicrouch. Now jump up — get the skis off the ground — and twist your body around and away from the pole. You should face the opposite direction when you land. This, however, will take a little practice. At first, the skis will probably feel heavy and clumsy.

You make the *jump turn* (similar to the hop turn) while schussing downhill at slow or moderate speed. The pole (or both poles) acts as support and pivot, enabling you to rise and turn in air.

The use of both poles is probably the most effective way to

New York State Department of Commerce photo

Gelandesprung is easy, exciting way to get over bumps on ski trail.

execute the jump turn. Place them near the tip of the downhill ski. Keep your skis parallel, and push your body upward, pivoting and twisting around the poles. Your body should be at an angle, legs outstretched, as you pivot around the poles. Land in a low crouch to absorb the shock, and edge your skis into the hill to prevent slipping downward.

Gelandesprung is a pole vault jump used to clear obstacles or bumps. From a crouching position, you swing both poles forward. Place your hands firmly on the tops of the poles, and set the poles into the snow near the top of the bump. Then throw yourself forward, and try to rise above the poles with your arms stretched out. Both knees should be pulled upward to your chest, and your skis should be close together as you float through the air. When you land, sink into a crouch position to better absorb the shock.

Cornice jumping, jumping off the edges of snow crests, is done in the same way as the gelandesprung. Keep your weight forward far enough so that your body and skis are parallel to the pitch of the slope.

Sun Valley News Bureau photo

Ski instructor Don Alldred does a cornice jump at Sun Valley, Idaho. Note skis are parallel to slope's pitch.

8

For Speed, Try Downhill Racing

When you've mastered the basic and advanced maneuvers discussed in earlier chapters, you're ready to swoop down almost any hill along with the expert skiers. As you gain skill and confidence, you'll find yourself improvising on the fundamentals. You're now developing your own style of skiing.

This is as it should be, for while we all must learn the fundamentals, our individual tastes and desires set us apart from others. How well we use the initial training is what separates the experts from the novice, the champions from the also-rans.

The alpine events — downhill and slalom racing — are skiing contests that can be enjoyed by young and old, men and women. In both events you use the basic and advanced maneuvers, along with your own variations.

Downhill racing is done on a course of from 1 to 5 miles. The course is marked at various points with control gates through which you pass. These control points more or less check your speed. Except for passing the required control points, you select your own course for getting downhill. Since time counts for every-

Sun Valley News Bureau photo

These expert skiers are having fun skiing over moguls, skier-made bumps in the snow. But unprepared skiers can be quickly upended by moguls.

thing in downhill racing, the shortest route you can safely travel is the fastest way.

For sheer speed, downhill racing is the most thrilling of the alpine sports. While speed is also essential in slalom, your main objective in slalom racing is to pass successfully through a series of gates.

Speed is stressed in downhill racing, and the steeper the hill, the more attractive and hazardous becomes the downhill run. At speeds of up to 60 miles an hour, downhill racers enjoy much the same nerve-tingling excitement that stirs the race car driver.

Entering ski races is one of the best ways to raise your skill and technique to higher levels. Downhill racing is demanding; it requires daring, skill and confidence. Unless you have these qualities, it is better to be a spectator instead of a competitor in downhill racing.

60

U. S. Forest Service photo

In downhill and slalom races, get off to a quick start. Split seconds determine the winner.

61

Swiss National Tourist Office photo

Swiss skiing champion Madeleine Chamot-Berthod passes a control point during a downhill race.

Training develops skill, and skill breeds confidence, but daring is something that's hard to describe. I think of a daring skier as a good skier who skis fast, but not so fast that he loses control over his skis. The good skier never exceeds the limits of his ability. He eliminates all the elements of danger possible, and he's careful not to try anything foolhardy.

In training for downhill racing, try to develop your technique of stemming and parallel skiing. Keep your body's center of gravity forward, for your tendency to fall increases as you pick up speed. Use rotation — swing action of your shoulders and hips — to make swift parallel turns. Knee action is important, because you'll hit all sort of unexpected bumps during the downhill run.

Downhill and slalom skiing call for coordination of your body and mind. Since speed is the essence of downhill skiing, you must be able to think fast. Keep your eyes on what's ahead, and make your decision to turn before you actually reach the turning point.

Austrian State Tourist Department photo

Austrian skiing champion Toni Sailer on a downhill run past admiring spectators.

To avoid chances of taking spills, make your turns on smooth places.

In downhill skiing, you'll frequently run into rough spots, bumpy snow piled up by skiers who turned in the same spot. Skiers refer to these bumps as moguls.

Moguls can give inexperienced skiers plenty of trouble. Unless you're prepared for these hard bumps, you're apt to take a nasty fall.

To ski over these skier-made bumps, keep your weight forward in a crouch position, and your knees working like pistons to absorb the shock. Check your balance when necessary by planting your poles in the snow. On heavily moguled terrain, try going around the bumps as well as skiing over them.

Another technique the downhill skier must master is skiing in deep snow. Since deep snow (also called powdered snow) is soft, your weight should be placed a little on your heels. This will raise the tips of your skis to the surface of the snow. If you maintain the same forward lean you've been trained to use during normal skiing conditions, the weight will force your skis down into the snow, and your body will pitch forward. In such a situation the skis would not respond to your turning motion. Instead, you'd get a cool face wash from the powdery snow.

To turn on hard-packed snow, you weight and push the outside ski to make the edges bite. But in deep snow, you should distribute your weight evenly on both skis rather than one foot at a time. If you try an ordinary stem movement in deep snow, your skis are liable to spread apart. Result? You take another tumble.

Touch your poles on each turn; pivot up and around.

While long traversing is fun in deep snow, it will slow you down on the turns. When skiing downhill in deep snow, stay as close as possible to the fall line.

The trick of deep-snow skiing is to keep a rhythmic, continuous forward movement. Keep the skis together, and continue the completion of each turn.

The secret of success lies in planning ahead. This is also true for downhill and slalom racing.

All skiers should make several practice runs down the course before the contest. Practice runs should be just that — test runs. Go down slowly first, and then faster, but never at top speed. Save the nonstop run until competition time. The main reason for making practice runs is to learn all you can about the course. Study and remember all you can about its landmarks, check the trouble spots, and pay particular attention to how other skiers make their downhill runs. Then make a definite plan for racing down the hill. Skiers who preplan their run not only save time skiing downhill, but they often end up as winners.

One more thing: get off to a quick start. Split seconds determine the outcome of downhill and slalom racing. The clock begins counting against you the moment the starter says, "Go!"

To get maximum forward thrust at the start, plant both poles securely near the actual starting line. Lean your body forward in an easy, springy position. Look ahead to the track beyond your skis. Follow the starter's countdown and launch yourself forward with an exploding motion.

Don't be discouraged if you should fall during a race. Get up as quickly as you can and get out of the way of other skiers. Then finish the race. The will to win is great, but a true athlete finishes the race even if he can't win.

G. H. Bass & Co. photo
A pair of typical downhill ski boots.

9

Slalom Calls for Controlled Skiing

The circus tightrope walker, the acrobatic gymnast, and the champion slalom skier all have common traits: they have agile minds and bodies, and they have great control over their reflexes and body movements.

Slalom is essentially a compulsory race; that is, it offers obstacles — gates — that require you to turn at definite spots.

Unlike the downhill race which calls for daring and speed, slalom racing emphasizes your twisting through various control gates. You're continuously turning as you make your way downhill. To do this, you must have absolute control over your skis, mind, and body. While it's often the reckless and the daring skiers who win downhill races, it's the technician, the master skier, who's victorious in slalom races.

I don't mean that speed doesn't count in slalom races; it does. The skier with the best time wins. But the slalom runner who can make continuous parallel turns in split seconds without braking will automatically gain in speed.

You should practice simultaneously for slalom and downhill,

U. S. Forest Service photo
Young skier shows excellent form as he makes sharp parallel christie turn during slalom race on Rainy Mountain Ski Area, Beaverhead National Forest, Montana.

Sun Valley News Bureau photo
Ski instructor Christian Pravda going through gates during a professional slalom race.

Robert St. Louis photo
Ski instructor Arthur G. Furrer makes high-speed slalom turn, his shoulder almost touching gate pole.

for each mode of racing complements the other. The quest for speed, so essential in downhill racing, is also necessary in slalom. And the skill and control over skis and body action demanded by the slalom racer will improve the skiing technique of the downhill racer.

The giant slalom, conducted over long and wide, rolling and steep hills, combines the features of slalom and downhill racing. Since its control gates are more widely dispersed than in the regular slalom, however, the giant slalom is in reality a controlled downhill race.

Gates (or flags) on a slalom course are set in pairs, and in alternating colors: red, blue, and yellow. The placing of the various pairs of flags depends entirely on the terrain and layout of the course. The racers must pass through all gates consecutively from start to finish. Checkers are stationed at various points along the course to spot mistakes by skiers. Mistakes are subject to penalties, which are added to skier's time. If the racer misses a gate, he must go back and go through it.

You may not practice on a slalom course before the race. This means that you must study and memorize the course as you go up to the starting gate.

Since you can't make a practice run, it's wise to pay close attention to how the course-setter makes his official run before the race starts. Compare your observations of the course with how the course-setter goes through the various gates.

Then, when you head down the course, think ahead to one, two, or three gates. Quick thinking and quick action go hand in hand during the slalom race.

When you ski in a slalom race, your body should be in a semi-crouch position with your knees bent. Some skiers use poles to aid in making turns, but unless you're an accomplished downhill or slalom skier, hold the poles to the rear.

How you approach a slalom gate or flag depends greatly upon the character of the course. For success in slalom, though, you should rely entirely upon the parallel christie. Other turns will slow you down.

On all turns, push the inside ski slightly ahead, and aim for the shortest and fastest line between gates. For a perfect high-speed slalom turn, your shoulder should almost brush the gate pole.

Slalom racing demands an excellent sense of balance and co-ordination of mind, body, and skis. The skier who trains and develops himself into a good slalom skier is well on his way to becoming a fine all around skier.

10

Touring: Rendezvous with Nature

Riding the tow to the top of the hill, and then schussing down at breakneck speed, is great fun, but downhill skiing is only one of many phases of this wonderful winter sport.

Touring, or cross-country skiing as it is also called, is one of the most stimulating and healthful phases of skiing. (In the next chapter we shall discuss cross-country skiing as long-distance racing.)

Touring is simply hiking on skis, and every skier should get in several touring trips a season. Touring the countryside on skis is one of the most pleasant ways of gaining healthful exercise along with a deep sense of appreciation of the wonders of nature. Touring is your rendezvous with nature.

Too many skiers never get beyond the evergreen trees that line the resort ski slopes. They're lazy.

To be a good all around skier, you must develop your skills in varied and unfamiliar terrain. You must get off your favorite slopes and into the heart of nature.

When touring, you'll have a chance to use every kind of skiing maneuver you've learned. You'll walk on level ground, climb hills and mountains, schuss downhill, make stem turns, and brake your descent with the snowplow. You'll do all these and other maneuvers under pleasant and leisurely conditions.

To get the utmost enjoyment out of touring, make definite plans before you start. Don't ramble all over the countryside without any goal in mind. Decide where you want to go, but be sure you can reach that goal and return without any difficulty.

You should never go on a ski tour alone. Always have a companion with you, and always let someone know where you're going, and when you expect to return. For a pleasant day, go on a ski tour with your family, friends, or school chums.

At first, plan short ski tours. Then, as you gain experience, extend these excursions.

U. S. Forest Service photo

Skiers head for picnic along snow-mantled trails of Vermont's Green Mountain National Forest. Ski tourists carry food, drinks, first-aid kit in rucksack.

U. S. Forest Service photo
Group of touring skiers hit Anvil Lake Ski Trail, Nicolet National Forest, Wisconsin.

Touring is fun, but it can become dreary and tiresome if you travel too fast. Move along at an easy pace, and stop frequently to rest and enjoy the scenery. When you stop, don't sit in the snow, but remain standing on your feet. You can relax leaning on your poles. Or you can rest on a log or tree stump; just be sure to brush away the snow before you sit.

The outfit used by the touring skier differs little from what the recreational downhill skier uses. Skis, boots, poles, and clothes remain the same. The ski hiker, however, may want to include a map and compass, sun goggles, and a rucksack for carrying food and first-aid equipment.

If you've never carried a rucksack, it's a good idea to try skiing with one before you embark on your cross-country trip. Adjust the rucksack to fit your back comfortably. You'll find you must maintain a good forward lean; otherwise the rucksack will pull

73

you backward on the heels of your skis. Falling with a rucksack can be clumsy.

Pack only what you need. Take only light food, such as sandwiches, fruits, and chocolate bars, and a water canteen. You may carry noncarbonated fruit juices, but go light on canned goods; they're bulky and heavy.

Warning: Don't eat too much! Touring will work up your appetite, but an overstuffed skier is dangerous to himself. He tires fast, takes spills, and becomes a burden to his fellow tourists.

Ski hikers frequently wear too much clothing. Then, when the going gets heavy, they sweat, peel off excessive clothing, get chilly, and end up with a cold or worse.

It's a good idea, though, to pack extra mittens in case your first pair gets wet. An extra sweater may be packed, since the temperature drops at higher elevations. Always wear enough

U. S. Forest Service photo
Last skier in group eyes trail before following touring companions in Olympic National Forest, Washington.

clothing to keep out the cold and yet not enough to make you perspire. A good, simple rule of thumb is: when you're climbing, take off clothes, and when you stop or come downhill, put some on.

Bring along a camera to record the wonderful sight of snow-capped mountains, white-dressed evergreens, and animal tracks. A showing of ski-tour movies is guaranteed not to bore your friends. A warning about cameras: photographic equipment can be heavy, so don't load yourself down with excess weight.

When touring in a group, have the most experienced skier be the leader. He selects the trail and leads the party in single file. Another strong skier should bring up the rear.

If you go ski touring in mountainous areas, be on the alert for avalanches — snow slides. There are only a few places in the East where you have to worry about avalanches, but in the West the danger of avalanches is more prevalent.

Avalanches may start on any slope of 22 degrees or steeper. Once you realize that it's possible to ski on slopes of 35 degrees — and occasionally on steeper gradients — you understand the possible consequences. My best advice is to stay away from avalanche-prone areas.

To guard against avalanches and to insure the safety of skiers, the U.S. Forest Service has snow rangers on duty in many national forest ski regions. They're hand-picked for their skiing ability, thoroughly trained to recognize avalanches in the making, and know how to bring them down in controlled slides. Avalanche control in the United States started in 1937 in Alta, Utah.

While on guard against avalanches, the snow rangers study the terrain, measure snow depths, and chart winds. They watch where and how the snow builds up to avalanche proportions, and they find ways to start slides. The daring rangers may ski across a steep slope until they trigger a slide, or they may blast with dynamite or shoot them down with recoilless rifles.

11

Cross-Country Racing

Cross-country racing is the hardest of all skiing events. Only boys in the best physical condition should participate.

Cross-country races are sometimes conducted for women, but I consider such races sheer stunts. Women skiers are marvelous and glamorous in downhill and slalom races, and of course, women and men, young and old, can and should enjoy ski touring.

When you look at cross-country skiers, you get the impression that all they do is to run across the ski trail. Running is only part of their technique.

The cross-country racer is an all around skier. During the race, whether it's for 5 or 30 miles, he has plenty of opportunities to make tricky slalom turns and speedy downhill runs.

Equipment used by the cross-country skier is light. He wears light clothing and in moderate weather races without gloves or headgear.

Modern cross-country skis are light and narrow — about 2¼ inches wide at the foot. They're somewhat shorter than other skis. Usually made of hickory or laminated wood, cross-country skis have *no* steel edges.

Cross-country poles are also light and — according to the racer's preference — a bit longer than downhill racing poles. Novice cross-country racers, however, should avoid using poles that are too long for comfort. Long racing poles may cause you to reach too high for effective pushing. They may also drag in the snow or get caught in brush.

Cross-country racers use Rottefelle or "rat-trap" bindings, which clamp the boot down securely at the toe, allowing free up-and-down movement of the heel.

Lightweight boots are extremely valuable to the cross-country skier. They're cut almost as low as oxfords. This gives the racer maximum control over his skis. Downhill boots are too stiff and heavy for cross-country running.

Training for cross-country racing begins *before* snow covers the ground. As soon as you feel the flow of the cool, exhilarating autumn air, begin your conditioning.

Jog along at first, increasing the speed as you get more accustomed to running. Short distances, not over two to three miles, several times a week are far more beneficial than extensive and exhaustive runs. After several weeks of conditioning, you can increase the distance you run.

Cross-country racing calls for endurance. The successful cross-country skier learns early to pace himself and save his strength for the final mile sprint. To get best results from your conditioning, maintain a steady pace throughout the runs.

The cross-country skier performs more muscular activity than does the long-distance runner who travels over a smooth track. So the cross-country skier gets more winded and tires quickly unless he's in good physical condition. Proper breathing, which is developed during preseason conditioning, lets the cross-country runner maintain his vigorous pace without becoming breathless.

When the snow falls, transfer your training to skis. Begin slowly. First accustom your feet and legs to the narrow skis; then step up the pace. Try to practice every day. Avoid long periods of inaction during the training period.

Running on cross-country skis requires finely developed bal-

Swiss National Tourist Office photo
Skiers "pass the baton" in cross-country race by touching team-mates on back.

ance and rhythm. Your body must be centered directly over the narrow skis. If you sway out of balance, you miss your rhythmic forward motion.

The novice cross-country racer can develop his balance and rhythm by spending about 30 minutes each day running without poles. That way you learn to thrust your body forward with your feet, a technique essential for the forward motion of the cross-country racer.

The first thing a novice skier learns is how to walk correctly on skis. The cross-country racer has refined the walking maneuver so that he not only walks, but he also slides and runs on skis.

The proper posture for cross-country racing is a forward, half-crouch position. Bend your knees so that they can kick your body forward at each step.

Poling action is important in cross-country racing. During the forward swinging action of your arms, bring the top of the pole

A-Foto A/S, Oslo, photo

Famed Norwegian cross-country racer Harald Grønningen shows proper cross-country running technique of high poling action, driving legs, and rhythmic forward motion.

up almost level with your face. On the downward swing, plant the pole firmly in the ground and give yourself a hard forward thrust. Your arms and poles should move forward and backward close to your body in a natural arc. Don't grip the poles too tightly; a tight hand can become tiring.

When practicing cross-country racing, pick out terrain in which you can not only slide on level ground but also run uphill and race downhill.

The toughest part of cross-country skiing is going uphill. How well you master your hill-running technique often decides the outcome of a race.

Most cross-country racers attack a hill head on. While running on level ground, your strides are long, but when you run uphill

80

the strides become shorter and faster. Plant the skis hard into the track, shorten your stride, and increase the rhythmic forward drive at the very moment you begin the incline. The key to good hill running is being able to maintain the low, forward-leaning body position and full knee drive. If you straighten up, which you're apt to do when you become tired, you'll loose the forward momentum.

Try to avoid using the herringbone when going uphill in a cross-country race. A herringbone will slow you down and tire you. If, however, the terrain forces you to change your running technique, try a half herringbone.

The half herringbone is used by cross-country racers and other skiers to help prevent backslip on gentle to moderate slopes in both straight uphill climbing and traversing.

You perform the half herringbone with one ski in the herringbone position, the other pointing in the direction you want to travel. Use the poles for support to prevent the ski pointed uphill

Austrian State Tourist Department photo

Slalom courses of IX Winter Olympics in Innsbruck, Austria, 1964. Notice the sharp twists.

from backslipping while you advance the other ski. As the slope gets steeper, increase the amount that the herringbone ski is angled and edged into the slope. You may think that a cross-country racer rests during the downward glide. Not so. You're racing against time, and you must use every chance to gain speed. On downhill runs, which are normally not very steep or long, dig both poles into the ground to gain more speed. On steep hills where double-poling is unnecessary, however, you do get a moment or two to catch your breath. Then, the moment you come to the bottom of the hill, you should again be off and running.

Ideal cross-country courses are laid out in terrain that gives the skiers about one-third flat ground, one-third uphill, and one-third downhill. The trails are marked by flags, and at various points are first-aid and food stations and checkers.

Cross-country ski races are races against time. Each competitor starts 30 seconds after the previous one. When one runner overtakes the runner ahead, he cries, "Track!" The man in front must go to the side and let the faster racer pass.

One of the more exciting variations of cross-country racing is the relay race. Four racers compose a team, each skier usually racing over the same course. In international competitions, such as the men's 40-kilometer cross-country relay, each skier covers 10 kilometers. Unlike track races, where relay runners pass batons, a ski relay racer must slap his teammate on the back before the next man can start.

G. H. Bass & Co. photo
Cross-country skiers use lightweight, low-cut boots that are clamped to skis at toes.

82

12

The Big Jump to Ski Jumping

The most spectacular event in skiing is jumping. It thrills not only the spectator but also the jumper.

Ski jumping demands agility, good balance, quick reaction, and steel nerves.

First, though, you must be a good all around skier who can handle himself on any kind of difficult slope. If you're a good downhill skier, chances are you can also develop into a good ski jumper.

Secondly, no matter how experienced you are as a downhill skier, ability alone doesn't make you a ski jumper. You must be filled with determination to soar like an eagle. In downhill skiing, you're safe with both feet on the ground. But, when ski jumping, you're all alone in space. There can be no hesitation; once you start down the inrun, there's no turning back. If you have this most important prerequisite — determination — only then may you take up ski jumping.

Ski jumpers use heavier and longer skis than do downhill skiers, but young children should start jumping on their regular down-

New York State Department of Commerce photo

Ski-jump training should begin early and progress gradually. Instructor, out of photo to left, keeps close watch.

hill skis. Boys of high school and college ages should use jumping skis, which are usually made of laminated hickory with plastic-finish bottoms. Three grooves on the bottoms help keep jumping skis on a straight track.

To determine the proper length for your jumping skis, stand erect and stretch your hands upward. The tip of your jumping skis should reach about four inches *above* your outstretched fingers.

Jumping boots must be both light and flexible, allowing you to get proper forward lean during the flight, and cushion the impact upon landing.

Bindings are toe plates with a cable going around the heel of the boot. The bindings should be so adjusted that your jumping ski hangs balanced horizontally from the toe plate.

Begin your ski jumping career on small hills. Don't let anyone dare you to try the big hills too soon. That would be foolhardy; you might get badly hurt.

Almost any hill clear of trees, rocks and brush can be made into a jumping hill. Be certain that the grade is not too great — a gentle slope of not more than 25 degrees at the steepest point is satisfactory.

The practice jump can be made of packed snow. A two-foot-high jump is tall enough to launch your jumping career. When building your own ski jump, remember that landing must be made on the slope. A flat landing gives a terrific impact which can result in falls and injuries.

Before you jump, make sure that the hill is clear of dogs and spectators. Never jump alone; always have at least one companion with you.

When you stand at the top of the ski-jump platform, take a deep breath and then throw yourself forward down the inrun in an upright position and gradually sink into a very low crouch (spring position) as you approach the take-off. Skis are close together, feet flat on the skis. Your hands are held forward of your bent knees in a natural, restful position.

As the ski tips reach the end of the jump, you straighten up with a powerful upward and forward leap. Swing your arms

U. S. Forest Service photo

This is the spectacular Olympic 80-meter ski jump at Squaw Valley, Tahoe National Forest, California.

forward, straighten out your knees, and keep your feet flat on the skis. This lift or "sats" is one thing every skier must perfect in order to become a skilled jumper.

Once you're in the air, keep your feet close together and your skis parallel. Lean forward at the ankles and hips. The amount of forward lean depends upon the jump; the longer the jump, the greater the forward lean.

Use your arms to maintain balance. Don't flutter them like a bird in a hurry, but hold them fairly steady. If you feel you're leaning too far forward, rotate your arms backward; if leaning too far back, rotate them forward.

As your momentum slows down, you prepare for a landing. Your body straightens out, and your eyes seek out a landing spot. Just before landing, raise your ski tips so they don't touch the snow first, or you'll suffer a serious fall. Maintain a forward lean upon landing; too much weight to the rear will throw you off balance and into a fall.

German Information Center photo

Mase Bolkart of West Germany displays fine aerodynamic style in jumping great distance on big hill.

State of New Hampshire photos

Skiers on these two pages and the following one demonstrate three phases of jumping on mighty 181.5-foot Nansen Ski tower at Berlin, New Hampshire. Skier at left is in proper crouch position as he swoops down in run. Above, another jumper is airborne immediately after take-off. The jumper on the next page displays perfect style as he soars confidently out into space, jumping 250 feet.

Upon impact, advance one ski slightly into what skiers call a "telemark" position. With knees bent, this position will absorb the shock of landing.

In a perfect landing, your skis should be close together. Too often, jumpers land with their legs apart in cowboy fashion, or with the heels of the skis touching down first. Avoid these mistakes early in your jumping career; faulty landings will score heavily against you later in competition.

Complete the jump by making a parallel christie turn on the outrun.

Ski jumping is a brief sporting event. Perhaps not more than 15 seconds pass between the time you enter the inrun and complete your christie turn at the bottom. Actual flight time may last two or three seconds.

A fall in ski jumping is as spectacular as the ski jump itself. A gasp goes up from the crowd, and parents anticipate the worst.

G. H. Bass & Co. photo
Typical boot of type worn by ski jumpers.

91

The uninitiated should know however, that every jumper falls many times — yet ski jumpers seldom get hurt.

As a ski jumper, you should learn early in your career how to fall without getting hurt. When falling down a ski-jumping hill try to skid or slide your relaxed body with arms outstretched. Keep your skis close together, flat on their side so they won't dig into the snow. Before ski jumping, remove hard objects from your pockets.

It takes long and determined training before you make an errorless flight, but don't rush yourself. Skill and confidence come only from good training. Study the form and styles of the experts, listen to and heed their advice. When you win their approval and can jump with complete concentration and confidence, then you're ready for the big hills.

Ski-Jumping Hill

1. Start
2. Inrun
3. Take-off
4. Landing area
5. Outrun

13

Ski Safely!

Skiing is fun, stimulating, and healthful, but the careless skier can turn a pleasant skiing session into a nightmare. Whether you're a beginner or an expert, you're responsible for the safety of yourself and others on the ski trail. To ski safely, you must use common sense and common courtesy.

Many skiing accidents could have been prevented if the victims had been able to ski under control, which means turning and stopping at will.

Ski fever is highly contagious, and millions of Americans now schuss down the slopes on weekends. The sad part of this happy picture, however, is that too many of them have never taken the trouble to learn even the basic skiing maneuvers. They seem to think that all you have to do to become a skier is to snap on a pair of boards and sail madly downhill.

Book learning is fine, but you can't merely read this book and then expect to go out and schuss down the slopes like an expert. You must practice your ski hobby often and well until you can pass the test: *Always ski in control.* It's a good idea to augment your book learning by, if possible, taking lessons from a certified ski instructor. For names of certified ski instructors in the area where you plan to ski, write to the United States Ski Association, The Broadmoor, Colorado Springs, Colorado.

Many injured skiers have been brought to safety and received medical aid by a group of Good Samaritans called the National Ski Patrol System. The more than 5,700 members of the National Ski Patrol System, an affiliate of the United States Ski Association, are on the job at ski centers throughout the nation. They help to prevent accidents on the ski slopes, and they give first aid to injured skiers without charge. Each patrolman is a competent skier who has successfully completed several Red Cross first-aid courses. When patroling a ski area they are as responsible for accident prevention as they are for aiding an injured skier.

Ski patrolmen are the lifeguards of the ski trails. At the end of the day, they make a final sweep of all ski runs to see that no one is left out overnight.

There are many safety do's and don't's for skiers. I'll mention only the more important ski safety rules here, but there are others which you will come to recognize by applying a little common sense.

• *Ski under control* — Learn to stop soon enough to avoid trouble. Ski on difficult runs only when you are able to control your skiing. Avoid deep snow until you learn how to handle it.

• *Right of way* — The person skiing downhill has the right of way. When two skiers are moving downhill, courtesy suggests that the lower skier has the right of way; however, he should not cut across the slope in the path of a skier above him. When the lower skier is standing still, the upper skier has the right of way. When starting down, be sure to look back up the slope to avoid moving out in front of the skier above you. When overtaking another skier call, "Passing on your right," or, "Passing on your left." Skiers approaching each other across the hill should pass to each other's right to avoid collision. Regardless of these courtesy rules, all skiers should be aware of beginners who may not be accustomed to proper skiing procedures.

• *Sitzmarks* — If you fall, the dent you make in the snow is

Sun Valley News Bureau photo

These four skiers zooming through the powder demonstrate an important principle:
never ski alone in remote areas, when touring, or when making difficult runs.

Sun Valley News Bureau photo

Famed skier Sigi Engl makes spectacular run in deep powder while keeping his skiing under perfect control.

called a "sitzmark." Fill in all your sitzmarks with snow. Stamp down the snow with your skis and smooth out the area so the hole won't trip up another skier. Filling in your sitzmark is a basic responsibility of every skier on any slope.

- *Stay where you belong* — Novices on expert terrain menace themselves and the experts, and the experts should stay away from the novice slopes, except when they act as instructors.

- *Don't ski alone* — Never ski alone in remote areas, when touring, or when skiing difficult runs. Ski jumping alone is sheer madness. Three skiers are better than two.

- *Proper equipment* — Safety on the slope is directly related to good equipment kept in good condition. Use safety straps linking the ski to your boot. Loose skis can cause serious injury to people below. Be sure that you shout a warning if a ski gets loose. Safety bindings may help you avoid injury. Choose clothing that's warm enough and affords good protection. Discomfort from cold will increase fatigue. Eat enough good food — but not too much. When touring, carry first-aid equipment. Never use a ringless pole. The willful and negligent use of skis or poles which causes personal injury to another person is considered assault.

- *Walking* — Don't walk on ski runs; the hole caused by your boot can cause a bad fall. Walk only at the edge of ski runs, and preferably on your skis.

- *Ski area* — Consult a map and ask questions about an area in which you'll ski so that you don't ski on slopes that are too difficult, or where there's avalanche danger. Heed avalanche signs and warnings of snow conditions.

- *Lift lines* — Wait your turn in the lift or tow line. Do not "crash" (cut into the line). If the line gets so long that it extends across the end of the trail, stand to the side of the trail in order to stay out of the way of skiers finishing their runs. (Line cutting is permitted only if you're in a ski class with your instructor, or if you're a ski patrolman on duty.)

- *Riding the lift or tow* — Ask questions about the lift or tow, and read instructions that may be posted. Don't wear loose clothing on any lift or tow, especially rope tows. Don't swing or bounce when riding a chairlift, and be sure to keep your skis pointed straight ahead with the tips up. Do not "snap" the Pomalift platters of the T-bars. The swinging bar may hurt another person or cause the lift cable to jump off the pulley. Don't ride any lift or tow with the straps of your ski poles around your wrist. If the poles catch onto something, the sudden jerk often causes a dislocated shoulder. Keep the straps in the palm of your hand or carry poles in your hand so you can let them go easily and quickly if necessary.

• *Runouts* — When you arrive at the bottom of the slope, don't stand in the flat runout at the end of the trail where skiers are moving very fast; ski flat runouts cautiously and under control; in these areas, the accident rate is high.

• *The "last run"* — The "last run" is the one during which people are most often hurt, because they are too tired to exercise proper control. Allow yourself plenty of time to complete your final run before the Ski Patrol sweeps the trails and closes the area for the day. When you get tired, stop skiing. Watch snow and weather conditions. Stop skiing when the shadows fall.

Have a good time, always skiing safely and courteously.

14

Training and Exercises

Everyone who takes part in athletics knows that in order to be a good competitor he must limber up and train his muscles before the sports season starts. Although skiing is a strenuous sport that demands an elastic and strong body, many skiers fail to do any kind of preseason training. Then, when the snow falls, they take the skis out for a trial run and find themselves out of shape, unable to make the simplest downhill run without puffing from lack of wind. Their legs are weak, and they take frequent spills, because the body lacks a sense of balance.

You should start your preseason ski training in September when the schools stir with excitement over football games and the coming basketball tournaments. While skiers who intend to enter competition should conduct a vigorous training program, the recreational skier can get along with less strenuous exercises. Both, however, should do as much walking as possible. As I have already emphasized, walking is the basic maneuver in skiing.

Most expert skiers engage in other sports. This enables them to keep in shape throughout the year. When winter starts, they're

Dr. Americo A. W. Favale photos

Skipping rope improves your agility and stamina.

well prepared for their favorite skiing event — downhill, slalom, cross-country, or jumping.

Off-season sports that are available to the skier are swimming, water polo, soccer, track and field events (especially running and jumps), Trampoline and tumbling, volleyball, and bicycling.

To help you limber up for the ski season, I suggest you conduct a regular program of conditioning exercises, as illustrated in the accompanying photographs.

100

Straddle jump conditions you for cross-country skiing.

Toe touch toughens you for strenuous bending.

1. *Skip rope* to improve agility and stamina. Vary skip positions from standup to crouch. Change pace, slowing down and speeding up.

2. *Straddle jump* for cross-country conditioning. Feet together, place hands on hips. Jump off the ground, land with legs spread in a long stride. Repeat rapidly, alternate left, right leg forward.

3. *Toe touch* from waistline. Raise arms full overhead, bend

101

Dr. Americo A. W. Favale photos

Trunk twist strengthens muscles essential in various turns.

Deep-knee bends develop leg stamina for downhill runs.

trunk forward and down, keeping knees straight, touching fingers at ankles. Bounce and touch fingers to toes. Return to position of attention.

4. *Trunk twist* strengthens body muscles essential to the various turns, parallel christie, wedeln, and so on. Place your feet 24 inches apart, flat on the ground (or floor), hands on hips. Twist trunk slowly, far as possible to left, then right. At end of each movement, give an extra twist with shoulders.

5. *Deep knee bends* develop leg stamina for downhill runs. Hands

102

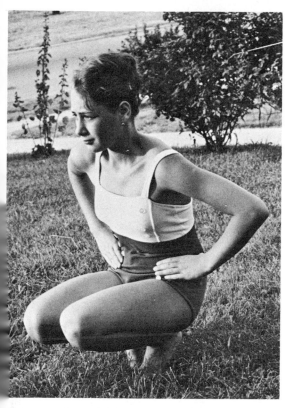

Duck waddle is excellent hip and leg conditioning for bumpy-trail skiing.

Bicycle is good exercise for strengthening stomach muscles.

on hips, feet together, flat on ground. Squat down as low as possible at least 20 times.

6. *Duck waddle* is excellent hip and leg conditioning for bumpy-trail skiing. Squat low, hands on hips, weight on toes: walk forward and backward, sidestep left, sidestep right. Do same with heels on ground (or floor).

7. *Bicycle* for stomach muscles. Lie on back, raise body and legs. Move legs in slow, bicycle fashion, toes pointed.

8. *Bongo board* develops balance as it tones leg muscles. Shift

Dr. Americo A. W. Favale photo

Bongo board develops balance as it tones your leg muscles.

weight from one leg to the other to get rolling action. Try squatting as you master the standing exercises. Bongo boards and rollers can be bought in most sporting-goods stores. You can, however, use any board and you can make your own roller from an evenly rounded log, keg or drum.

One last exercise: Push away from the table! Exercising will make you hungry, but don't stuff yourself, especially with potatoes and similar starchy foods. Fat skiers make big sitzmarks!

15

Ski Clubs

Skiers are a happy lot, and skiing is filled with energy and gladness. No other outdoor activity offers as many chances as skiing does for comradeship and mutual enjoyment of a stimulating hobby.

Skiers, like most Americans, enjoy getting together to rehash their experiences. Once the ski runs have closed for the day, you'll find the happy, tired skiers recounting and bragging a bit about their wonderful day.

As joiners, skiers have their own clubs. These ski clubs can be purely social or strictly athletic. Most combine both aspects. Many high schools and colleges have active ski clubs.

Membership in a ski club not only provides members with good fellowship, but also gives them a chance to take part in many programs that will aid them in their ski-training program.

Ski clubs conduct special skiing programs for juniors — skiers under eighteen years old. Special meetings, instruction, and competition are available for junior skiers.

Training camps are conducted for both juniors and seniors.

Most training camps, though, are for juniors, who receive instruction in competitive skiing from champion skiers. These camps do a great deal in helping to build future ski champions.

Preseason conditioning programs, including "dry-land" skiing and hikes, are conducted by ski clubs.

Clubs provide their members with special showings of ski-instruction films and other educational materials that help them improve their skiing.

Through ski clubs, you may get special prices on skiing magazines and ski books.

Ski club members are frequently entitled to discounts on skiing equipment at sporting-goods stores.

Many ski clubs publish attractive bulletins that keep you notified of club activities, ski conditions and facilities, and personal items on members.

Reduced-rate tours to ski resorts are arranged by many ski clubs.

Some ski clubs operate on a year-round basis with a full schedule of winter and summer activities.

The United States Ski Association (USSA) is the focal point for amateur ski clubs in the United States. Formed in 1904 by a group of interested skiers who wished to see skiing grow in an orderly way in this country, the USSA (formerly the National Ski Association — NSA) is the official voice of organized amateur skiing in the United States.

The United States Ski Association, with headquarters at The Broadmoor, Colorado Springs, Colorado, fosters the over-all development of junior competition in the United States. It sees that the Junior National Ski Championships are staged according to the rules.

The USSA aids schools in establishing ski programs by setting standards for ski programs within the schools. As the result of this program, many high schools have added skiing to their physical education curriculum.

The Association devises and promotes ski programs (other

U. S. Forest Service photo

These touring skiers make it up a hill with the herringbone climb.

U. S. Forest Service photo

Members of ski clubs get instruction from expert skiers and participate in many athletic and social activities.

than competitive) for people of all ages — such things as slope classification, special ski trips, preseason preparation, and advice to the beginning skier.

The USSA also builds and maintains shelters in remote areas to provide shelter for individuals on overnight hiking and ski-touring trips.

The United States Ski Association is, of course, responsible for selecting, training, equipping, and transporting of United States teams for international competitions, including the Winter Olympics and the world ski championships staged by the FIS — Federation of International Ski.

In addition to working closely with the United States Olympic Association and the FIS, the United States Ski Association works actively with and supports the Amateur Athletic Union, the National Collegiate Athletic Association, the National Ski Patrol System, and Ski Industries of America.

Most amateur ski clubs are affiliated with the United States Ski Association through membership in one of the seven divisions which make up the Association. These regional divisions conduct active skiing programs for their members. The regional associations sanction ski meets and supervise the selection of teams that each year participate in the National Junior Championships.

If you wish to join an established amateur ski club, and don't know of one in your vicinity, you can write to the USSA division in your area. To help the division locate the club most suited for you, include in your letter your age and the type of club you would be interested in joining. (While most ski clubs devote their activities to all phases of the sport, some clubs limit themselves to jumping or downhill, for example.) Address your letters to the Executive Secretary of the appropriate USSA division. Their addresses are:

Northern Rocky Mountain Ski Association (NRMSA)
1320 Hauser Boulevard
Helena, Montana

Intermountain Ski Association (ISA)
428 Downington Avenue
Salt Lake City, Utah

Far West Ski Association (FWSA)
P.O. Box 2431
San Francisco, California

Pacific Northwest Ski Association (PNSA)
Box 434
Yakima, Washington

United States Eastern Amateur Ski Association (USEASA)
98 Main Street
Littleton, New Hampshire

Central U.S. Ski Association (CUSSA)
205 East Front Street
Traverse City, Michigan

Southern Rocky Mountain Ski Association (SRMSA)
520 Boston Building
Denver 2, Colorado

Many young skiers who have become quite proficient in their hobby join the National Ski Patrol System. The System is made up of men and women, all volunteers, who are devoted to rescue and first-aid treatment of injured skiers throughout the United States. Members are divided into three categories: junior ski patrolmen, senior ski patrolmen and national ski patrolmen.

All ski patrolmen have completed various Red Cross first-aid courses and have demonstrated their skill in skiing under the most adverse conditions. Each year, in order to continue in the program, they must take refresher courses and demonstrate their skiing skill.

Many ski club members are also volunteer ski patrolmen. For information about this worthwhile program, write to the National Ski Patrol System, 828 Seventeenth Street, Denver, Colorado.

Among the better organized skiing programs for young people are those conducted by the Boy Scouts and Girl Scouts.

Scouts who try out for and succeed in obtaining the Merit Badge for Skiing can consider themselves among the best skiers on any slope.

16

Where to Ski

Not too many years ago, skiing was popular in only a few states where snowfall was heavy and it was enjoyed by comparatively few courageous enthusiasts.

Today, all this has changed.

More and more people are discovering that skiing is fun for the whole family — a sport the family can enjoy together. While no one knows for certain, educated guesses are that over four million Americans now consider themselves skiers.

Today you don't have to live in a snow-belt state to enjoy skiing. With the aid of artificial snow-making machines, you can now enjoy skiing in warmer states.

Skiing is big business. Americans spend about $45 million on equipment alone each year. Many more millions of dollars are spent at plain and fancy ski resorts.

To meet the increase in skiers, new resorts spring up almost overnight near slopes that offer some of the world's finest ski conditions. Other ski resorts are constantly adding to their accommodations.

New York State Department of Commerce photo
Skiing family enjoys a picnic at Big Tupper Ski Center in New York State's Adirondack Mountains.

A ski club generally keeps a complete file on ski resorts in its own state or geographical region. The clubs frequently get reduced rates and other special privileges for their members who visit certain ski resorts.

If you read advertisements in newspapers and magazines, you'll have no problem in locating ski areas in your vicinity.

Travel agencies will not only tell you where the skiing areas are, but they'll also gladly make all the arrangements for a ski vacation.

Not to be overlooked as places to ski are the national forests, which offer some of the best skiing in the country. In all, 167 ski areas, including more than 80 percent of the major ski areas in the West, are partly or entirely on national forest land.

17

A Short History of Skiing

Scandinavians are credited with being the world's first skiers. Skis 2,500 to 5,000 years old have been found in bogs of Norway, Sweden, and Finland.

Today, most skiers look toward Norway as the ancestral home of modern skiers. Through the ages, skis have played an important part in the life of the Norwegian people. Without skis, the Norwegians would have been snowbound for several months each winter, but with skis they could attend to all kinds of work which involved moving about.

Skis were mentioned in Norse mythology, where Ull was the ski god and Skade the ski goddess.

Snorri, the Icelandic saga writer, described Norwegian Vikings as good skiers. The first skier to reach our shores probably was a crew member of a Viking ship Leif Ericson used when he discovered America in the year 1000. Leif's brother-in-law, Thorfinn Karlsefni, who spent several winters on American shores, no doubt used skis to get around.

Up to 1850, Norwegians used only a toe strap on their skis and one long stick which they used as a brake when skiing downhill. Then the people of Telemark introduced ski bindings, and now it became possible to make ski jumps and downhill slides at great speed.

With the introduction of bindings, the Norwegians began to make slalom runs. Slalom is an ancient Norse word, made up of two syllables: "sla" means a slope and "lom" means a trail. Today, slalom indicates a steep trail which leads through several gates.

In 1206, when Norway was ravaged by a civil war, the two-year-old son of King Haakon III was saved from the enemy by quick action of two of the king's fastest skiers. They carried the child as they skied across the mountains. This saga is commemorated through the great marathon race from Lillehammer to Rena

Austrian State Tourist Department photo
Here's the downhill course for men during the 1964 Winter Olympics at Innsbruck, Austria.

Vermont Development Department photo
Both competitive and recreational skiing have made great gains in the U. S. since World War II.

every winter. The race is called the "Birch Leg Ski Race" and covers 35 miles across the mountains. It takes five to seven hours from start to finish.

In 1521, Swedish troops stretched animal skins between skis to transport their wounded, and thereby created the first stretchers.

Skiing was introduced into Central Europe via Austria in 1590, and subsequently to the Americas, Japan, Australia, New Zealand, and India.

At the close of the nineteenth century, many Norwegians emigrated to the United States and other countries, and a great number also went abroad in order to study at foreign universities. They discovered that skis were unknown everywhere. Many wrote home and asked that their skis be sent. But in America, they made their own skis on the farms.

By 1841, Norwegian-Americans were using skis in Wisconsin, and Scandinavian immigrants, trying their luck during the California gold rush, in 1849, used skis to get around the mining camps.

One miner who didn't find any gold, Norwegian-born John A. "Snowshoe" Thompson (born Jon Torsteinson Rui), made 90-mile treks on skis over the Sierra Nevadas carrying mail. (In the early days skis were called snowshoes; therefore the "snowshoe" nickname for Thompson.)

The first skiing competitions in the United States were organized by two Norwegian brothers, Mikkel and Torjus Hemmestveit, in the Midwestern states during the 1880's.

Many ski clubs were also formed by Norwegians, and in 1904 they joined with others to start the National Ski Association (now the United States Ski Association) in Ishpeming, Michigan.

It was not until after World War I, however, that skiing attained widespread popularity in the United States. The first downhill race was conducted by the Dartmouth Outing Club in 1926.

Skiing became an Olympic sport during the 1924 Winter Games at Chamonix, France. As was to be expected, the Scandinavians dominated the games.

The 1932 Winter Olympic games at Lake Placid, New York, gave skiing a tremendous boost in the United States. Thousands of Americans who previously had no inkling what skiing was all about, decided to take up this new winter hobby.

Ski resorts sprang up in many snow-decked mountain areas, and European ski instructors, especially those from Central Europe, came to the United States. They concentrated on the downhill and slalom techniques. American skiers were slow to accept the Nordic skiing events — jumping and cross-country racing.

The first United States downhill championship was at Warren, New Hampshire, in 1933; the first U.S. slalom championship in Seattle, Washington, in 1935; and the first woman's U.S. downhill championship was at Stowe, Vermont, in 1938.

During World War II, there were few competitive skiing events, and recreational skiing dropped considerably. The army trained young skiers for its special ski troops. One of America's greatest ski jumpers, Norwegian-born Torger Tokle, was killed leading his fellow ski troopers into action in the Italian alps.

116

Interest in both competitive and recreational skiing made strong gains after World War II, and the United States sent teams of fine young skiers to international events, including the Winter Olympic games.

In the 1952 Winter Olympics, at Oslo, Norway, a young Vermont housewife, Andrea Mead Lawrence, won two gold medals — in the slalom and the giant slalom.

When the Winter Olympics returned to the United States in 1960, at Squaw Valley, California, U.S. skiers failed to win any Olympic gold medals, but Penny Pitou won silver medals in the downhill and giant slalom, while Betsy Snite took the silver medal for the slalom.

Two young boys, William "Billy" Kidd of Stowe, Vermont, and James Heuga of Tahoe City, California, ended the United States' men's draught in the Winter Olympics by capturing second and third place in the men's slalom race at Innsbruck, Austria, in February 1964.

Only one girl, Jean Saubert of Lakeview, Oregon, won medals for the United States in the IX Winter Olympics at Innsbruck. The co-ed from Oregon State tied for second in the women's giant slalom after earlier having captured third place in the women's slalom race.

Winter Olympic ski races in 1968 will be held in Grenoble, France.

Sun Valley News Bureau photo

Ski instructor Rudi Tschabrun shows students the fine points of jump turn.

18

What Is Snow?

Snowflakes are formed from water vapor, at or below 32° Fahrenheit, without passing through the liquid water state. Newly fallen snow undergoes many changes on the ground. As the snow mass on the ground becomes denser, the snowflakes consolidate, and the entrapped air is expelled. These changes are caused by temperature, humidity, sunlight, and wind.

In general, the lower the temperature, the drier the snow and the less consolidation there is. As the temperature rises, snow tends to compact more readily. Temperatures above freezing cause wet snow conditions. Lowered night temperatures may turn wet snow into an icy crust.

The two characteristics of snow that are of most interest to the skier are:

1. *Carrying capacity* — Generally, when snow is packed hard, it will carry you on skis without difficulty. New, powdery snow will cause you to break through the surface snow. Although the carrying capacity of ice crust can be excellent, you'll have difficulty in moving because of the slippery surface.

2. *Sliding characteristics* — All-important to the skier are the sliding characteristics of snow. Wet snow will make the skis stick; dry, new snow makes gliding easier.

GLOSSARY

Binding — The harness that holds the boot to the ski.

Camber — The curved arch in a ski.

Christie — Short for christiania, a turn during which the skis are held parallel.

Cornice — An overhanging ledge of snow or ice.

Cross-country racing — A foot race on skis.

Downhill — An alpine ski race in which the competitors race against time over a downhill course.

Downhill ski — The ski which is on the downhill (lower) side of the skier.

Edging — The angling of skis into the snow to prevent slipping downhill.

Fall line — An imaginary line, the shortest distance downhill.

Gate — A pair of flags through which the skier must pass during downhill and slalom races.

Gelandesprung — A pole jump over snow bumps and obstacles.

Giant slalom — An alpine race, combining features of downhill and slalom racing.

Groove — Slot on the bottom of the ski to aid in straight steering.

Herringbone — A V-shaped method of climbing uphill on skis.

Hop turn — A quick-turn exercise in which the skier jumps up and twists his body around in a new direction.

Jumping — A ski event in which the skier, using heavier and longer skis, jumps into space on a specially designed jumping hill.

Kick turn — A method of changing direction on skis while standing stationary.

Mogul — A mound formed by pileup of snow from skiers' having made repeated turns in the same spot.

National Ski Patrol System — A nationwide organization of qualified skiers who volunteer their services as rescue workers on ski slopes.

Schussing — A straight downhill run without turns.

Sitzmark — The dent or hole a skier makes in the snow when he falls backward.

Slalom — An alpine skiing event in which the skier descends along a winding course, passing through a series of gates.

Snowplow — A basic maneuver for slowing down or stopping.

Snowplow turn — An inverted V-shape turn.

Stem turn — A basic turn performed by pushing skis outward at heels.

Touring — Hiking on skis.

Traverse — Skiing across a slope.

United States Ski Association — The national organization of organized amateur ski clubs in the United States.

Wedeln — A method of zigzagging downhill on skis.

Index

124

The Author

WILLIAM O. FOSS spent most of his youth
in Norway. When he returned to the United
States he was an accomplished skier. A veteran
of the U. S. Navy, he has also served as a trans-
lator-researcher for the Central Intelligence
Agency in Washington.

Mr. Foss is the co-author with Erik Bergaust
of *Helicopters in Action, Coast Guard in Action,* and *Marine Corps in Action.*